Cras[illegible] Jungle

Jim Alderson

Stanley Thornes (Publishers) Ltd

Originally published 1979 by Hutchinson Education

Reprinted 1990 by
Stanley Thornes (Publishers) Ltd
Ellenborough House
Wellington Street
CHELTENHAM GL50 1YW

99 00 / 20 19

ISBN 0 7487 0366 7

Set in IBM Pyramid

Printed and bound in Great Britain by
Martin's The Printers, Berwick.

Note

This is a true story about a plane crash in South America. It happened on 24 December 1971, when the plane ran into a storm. At 9000 feet above the Amazon jungle, it blew up.

Only one person survived the crash. This was a girl called Juliane Koepcke. She wrote down the story of how she found her way to safety, and this book follows closely her own words.

The publisher is grateful to *Stern* Magazine for permission to reproduce this adaptation.

1

I was feeling very happy that Christmas Eve. My mother and I were going home to see my father. He had a Christmas tree at home. He was waiting for us to get home to see it. I had never had a Christmas tree before, and I was feeling excited.

I got on the plane with my mother. I liked flying. I thought it was great fun. But my mother was not so happy. She was afraid of flying.

There were more than eighty people on the plane. I got a seat by the window so that I could see out. It was on row nineteen. My mother sat down next to me. I could tell she was still afraid.

We had to wait for the plane to take off. But that did not worry me. In my country, planes are always late. We were more than four hours late, but that was normal.

Everything else was just as normal, too. The take-off was good. We could see the sea below. It was very blue. The plane went up and up. We went over the tops of mountains.

Then we were given a meal. The air-hostesses were smiling. They always seem to be smiling. It makes the passengers feel safe. In fact some of the passengers were already asleep. My mother wasn't asleep, though. She was wide awake. She was still afraid. But that was normal too. I wasn't worried. I looked out of the window.

We could see the mountains far below. They were covered in snow. Then we flew over the jungle. It was very green and it seemed to have no end. It went on for miles and miles. It was all very beautiful. I was glad I had a seat near the window.

The air-hostesses came round to collect the dishes. They were still smiling. Everything was still just as normal.

But then things began to go wrong. Thick clouds came down. I could not see the land below. The wind grew stronger, and the plane began to shake. The shaking got worse. We were told to fasten our safety belts.

I was not afraid at first. This had happened to me before. I knew it was just the wind. You always get wind near the mountains.

But then the rain came too. It beat against the window. Suddenly the plane was thrown about all over the place. Bags and cases fell off the racks. Men and women began to scream. I looked out into the clouds. I saw a flash of lightning. It looked much too near the window. There were screams again from the people in the plane.

Suddenly I saw flames outside the window!

2

'I knew it! This is the end!' my mother cried. She had been in a storm once before. The plane had almost crashed. That was why she was now always afraid of flying. But now I was afraid as well. I held her hand tight.

I looked at the flames with panic. They were bright and yellow in the dark clouds. They shot out of the right wing of the plane.

I turned to look at my mother. But at that moment there was a great jolt. The jolt went right through the plane. I screamed and then I must have fainted.

The next thing I knew was that I was no longer inside the plane. I was out in the open air. But I was still tied into my seat. I was flying through the air!

I remember that I could hardly breathe. The seat belt was pressing on my chest. I remember that I was turning round and round in the air. I remember seeing the jungle way down below. I could see the trees. They looked like tiny plants. Lots and lots of tiny plants.

Then I fainted again.

3

I was woken by the rain. It was pouring down, as it does in the rainy season. It was still daylight and I could see the jungle all around me. But what was I doing here? I couldn't remember a thing.

Then I heard a clap of thunder. It all came back to me. The plane, the storm and the crash.

I was lying under my seat. But the seat next to mine was empty. My mother was not there. There was no trace of her. There was also no trace of the man who had sat next to my mother. He had still been fast asleep when the plane had made that great jolt. What had happened to them? Where were they? I felt dizzy. I could not think clearly.

I could not see any trace of the plane. All I could hear was the sound of frogs croaking and insects buzzing. There were trees everywhere. I was all alone in the jungle.

I did not feel in any pain, but I was too weak to get up. I was too weak to have a good look around. So I stayed under the seat all night.

Next morning I tried getting up. It took me a long time to move because I still felt so dizzy. I found I had lost a shoe and my glasses. But my dress was not torn. This was quite a surprise after such a fall.

A bone was sticking out from underneath my neck. It must have been my collar bone. It looked awful but it did not hurt me at all. That was quite a surprise. I had a big bump on my head as well, and a cut on my foot, but they did not hurt either. It must be the shock, I thought.

There was a little box near me. I picked it up and opened it. Inside were some toys and a Christmas cake. It was only then that I remembered it was Christmas Day!

I began to think about my father and the Christmas tree he had got for us. There he would be, spending Christmas on his own, thinking he had lost his whole family. I said to myself, 'He is not going to lose his daughter. I will stay alive, I will!'

But I knew my chances were slim. How could anyone stay alive in the middle of this jungle, miles from home? How could I survive?

4

I knew quite a lot about the jungle and its dangers. I had lived in it for two years with my parents. My father and mother worked with birds and animals as their job. They had told me all about the dangers of the jungle.

I knew that the worst animals were the small ones. I was not afraid of the jaguars, ant-eaters or wild pigs. I was more worried about the insects, spiders, ants, flies and mosquitoes.

My parents had told me that if you were lost in the jungle, you must always look for a river. A river always leads somewhere, just like a road. And people live on the river banks. If I could find some of the Indian tribes, I could get help from them. So I set off to look for a river to follow.

I did not eat the Christmas cake before I left. I tasted one small bit. It was very wet and tasted horrible. But I did find a bag of sweets. I would eat them later. They must have been somebody's Christmas present.

I found myself a stick. I used it to poke the

ground in front of me. I had one bare foot and one cut foot, so I did not want to step on any snakes, spiders or ants. At first I could only walk a few steps. I felt dizzy and the jungle kept spinning round and round.

Then I heard a sound. It was the sound I had been waiting for. It was the sound of running water. Perhaps I had found a river at last.

It was only a small stream. But it was clear and fresh, so I could drink from it. And this small stream must lead to a bigger stream. So I decided to follow it along and hope I came to a river with people living by it.

Rivers in the jungle do not flow straight at all. They are full of bends and loops. You can follow a river for miles and then find you are almost back where you started. But I knew it was death to take short cuts. The jungle is too full of danger. I must keep to the bank of the stream.

5

At last I came to a bigger river, but there was nobody living near it. I did not see any huts or any people. The animals by the river had never seen a human being before, I could tell. I could tell because they were not afraid of me. So I must be still a long way from help.

All the same, I had to follow the river so as not to get lost. There was no track beside it at all, and the bank was very difficult to follow. Big fallen trees kept blocking my way. Every so often I could not get past and had to cross over the river.

Then suddenly I heard the buzzing of flies. I followed the noise round a bend, and then I stopped. There was a row of seats from the plane. In the seats were three dead bodies. They were terribly cut and broken. The flies were crawling all over them. It was the most horrible thing I had ever seen. I felt sick all over.

I did see that my mother was not one of them. Then I just walked on in a daze. There was nothing else I could do. I could not help them now.

I was still carrying the sweets with me. So every now and then I ate a sweet from the bag. But I was not hungry at all. I saw fruit all round me, hanging from the trees. It all looked very beautiful, but I did not pick any fruit. It might be full of poison. In the jungle, so many beautiful things are full of deadly poison. My father had always told me this.

I kept tapping the ground with my stick. I kept watching out for spiders and snakes. After a time I saw that I had lost some of my sweets. They had fallen through a hole in the bag. But I did not care about that. I was still not hungry.

Then I heard a sound. A horrible sound of screeching. I knew that sound. Vultures! Vultures are always found near dead bodies. They must be eating the people from the crash. I tried to forget it, and walked on.

Later, I saw a bit of the plane. It looked like the cabin. There were wires everywhere, and a smell of petrol. I could just make out the number of the plane on the side. But I was glad I did not see any more bodies.

On the second and third days my cuts and insect

bites did not hurt me. But the skin on my back began to hurt. I was getting badly burned by the sun. The sun can be as bad as the rain in the jungle. I did feel a bit stronger now, even though I had eaten nothing but a few sweets. I don't know why.

Suddenly I heard the sound of planes. I shouted. I knew it was a waste of time, but I still kept shouting. 'Hello! Help!' I shouted again and again. 'Hello! Help!'

They must have been very close. But the pilots could not see me. I was hidden by the trees. I could not even see the planes. And I had nothing to signal with. So the planes just went away.

I was alone again.

6

I made myself start walking again. I walked until it was almost dark. Then I found a smooth spot on the river bank. I lay down. I tried to rest. But I did not get much sleep. I could hear things moving in the grass.

Suddenly, I felt something on my leg. Just a tickle at first. Then I felt it move. Something was crawling up my bare leg.

Did I dare to look down? It was a spider. A huge spotted spider. I shook my leg, and it ran off into the grass. I lay and shook, and waited for the dawn.

Next morning I set off again. I did not want to get lost, so I kept walking along the bank of the river.

But even the rivers are dangerous in the jungle. They have rapids and whirlpools. They can suck you under the water, and you drown very quickly. Tree trunks and big branches are swept along by the river. They are big enough to knock you out or even kill you. And you always find mosquitoes by a river. Billions of them. They bite like hell.

But worst of all are the little fish with sharp teeth. They are called piranha fish. I had heard all about them. They hunt in thousands. If they attack you, that is the end. In two minutes they can strip all the flesh off a man or a large animal. There would be nothing left but the bones floating down the river. They are the terror of the jungle. So what could I do about the cut on my foot? The piranha fish attack anything that is cut or open. They smell the blood. This made me afraid of the open cut on my foot. It was now half an inch deep and two and a half inches wide.

Then there were alligators in the river. They are cunning and greedy. Once they get you in their jaws, you are as good as dead. I was terribly afraid of them.

I remembered the sting rays as well. I knew there were sting rays in this jungle. They are full of poison. They lie on the banks of the river. 'If you step on a ray,' I told myself, 'that will be the end of you.' From then on I was even more careful.

Once I was so tired I lay down in the sand. I was

about to go to sleep. Then I saw five small alligators. They were next to me. They were still babies, only a foot long. I was not afraid of them because they were so small. But I knew their mother would be near. She would attack me if I fell asleep. She would drag me into the water. So I got to my feet, and set off again.

Later on, I found some ants blocking my way. Large ants, called fire ants, which drop down from the trees. There were thousands of them. I knew they were very dangerous, so I had to step into the river to get past them. The water came up to my hip. I pushed my way through the water for an hour but I only went a few hundred yards.

I was getting very tired. I did not think I could go on much longer.

7

In the middle of every day I had to keep stopping. It was so hot I could hardly move. It was not only hot but damp as well. It was like being in a hot steam bath.

Then it would pour with rain. The rain came down in sheets from the thick black clouds. There was lightning all over the sky. Claps of thunder shook the ground. This would happen every single day, as it was the rainy season. My dress was wet through most of the time.

That was not all. I was now sure that my collar bone was broken, because it was sticking right out of my neck. My eyes were all puffy. My head was covered with bumps from the crash, and my foot was badly cut. The shock had worn off, and I was in pain all over my body.

I had been walking now for almost six days. I was getting weaker. When I trod on an animal, I screamed. A scorpion or a snake could hide in the grass, but I was too tired to look out for them.

The mosquitoes and flies never left me alone. They

were always there, buzzing round my head all day long. The cut on my foot had got worse because of the insects. They kept biting at it. They made the cut bigger and bigger.

Then the flies began to lay eggs under my skin. It was a horrible thing to see in your own skin. I tried to dig the eggs out, but I had nothing to use, nothing like tweezers. So I had to leave the eggs to hatch out. What else could I do?

Out of the eggs came maggots. The maggots began to push their heads through my skin. I was nearly sick when I saw them. I was being eaten alive!

I began to get more worried about my arm. It looked terrible. The flies had stung it badly, and the maggots were getting bigger and bigger. 'My God,' I said to myself. 'If I am saved, they will have to cut off one of my arms.'

I needed to cover my bites, but what could I use? I had finished the sweets now, but I did not throw the bag away. It was made of cloth, so I tore it up into strips. I tried to cover the bites, but there were just too many. The bites still got bigger and bigger. I could not keep the insects off me. I was covered by them.

The worst thing was the pain in my arm. The maggots were crawling all over it. I had to do something about it. If I did not do something I would die. The maggots would eat me alive.

Then I thought of something I could do. I had a ring. It was a spiral one. I snapped it into sharp little bits and used them as tools. I began to scrape out the maggots from the cuts in my arms and legs. I looked at these insects. Each maggot was a quarter of an inch long.

I kept digging into my arm and leg with the bits of metal. It was terribly painful. And when I had got rid of one lot of maggots, the flies came back and laid more eggs. All the same I felt better. I was putting up a fight against these insects who were trying to eat me alive.

8

The next thing that hit me was a fever. I began to have strange dreams. My ears kept playing tricks on me. It was like being crazy. I felt I was going mad.

The bird calls began to play tricks on me. I thought I heard the sound of tame hens, but it was only a wild bird.

Then I heard the sound of a helicopter. Or, at least, I thought I did. Was this a trick again? No, I was sure it was a helicopter. But I could not see it. It must be flying above the clouds. I was angry. They had taken this long to come out and look, and then they flew too high to see below the clouds. How would they ever find the people from the crash?

There was nothing I could do to show them where I was. Nothing at all. The sound went away. The helicopter must have given up. I was left with only the flies and mosquitoes, and their bites. I sat down and kicked at the ground.

The life of the jungle went on all around me. The alligators, with their horrible thick skins, lay in the mud. Parrots and monkeys cried from the trees. Down in the mud, some big black frogs were hopping and jumping about. I thought I might eat one of the frogs, but I did not dare. I set off again, down the river.

I was getting tired, very tired. I had been walking now for nine days. But I knew I had to keep moving. If I stopped too long in one place I would die.

The river was running faster here. It often swept me off my feet. It just carried me along. It was a good job I knew how to swim. My father had made me learn. He had said, 'You never know. One day you might have to swim for your life in a jungle river.'

When night came, I looked for lights in the darkness. Indians in the jungle hang up oil lamps to keep off evil spirits. But I saw no trace of them at night. In the day I hoped to see Indians when they went hunting for fish with bows and arrows. But again, I saw nobody.

But I did at last see something which told me there were people about. It was about five o'clock in the afternoon. I could tell the time by the length of the shadows. It would be dark in one hour. I had to find a place to lie down for the night, and was looking down the river bank.

It was then that I saw a boat.

9

At first I thought the boat must be an old wreck. It was full of holes. I thought somebody had left it to rot. But when I looked again I saw that it was not a bad boat. In fact it was quite new, and made from good strong wood.

I was filled with hope. There must be human beings near by! Would I be saved at last? I could hardly believe my luck.

The boat was tied up to the bank of the stream. I could see a narrow track leading away from the bank. I went along it and found a little hut. It was made from branches of palm trees.

I walked up to the hut. I saw that it was new. The only thing inside was a plastic sheet. Under this sheet was a small motor and a can of petrol. The hut had a rough floor made of wood. When it was dark I lay down on this floor.

It was the first time I had a roof over my head for nine nights. But I could not get to sleep. The mosquitoes were still biting me. I kept listening for the sound of human voices. But this was a stupid thing to do. Nobody ever walked about in the jungle at night. Once I looked out and saw a light. But it was only the fireflies.

I tossed and turned, but could not sleep. The pain kept me awake, and I still hoped somebody might come in the night. I did not want to miss them. So I took the plastic sheet outside, and went down to the river bank. I used the plastic sheet to keep off the mosquitoes. Then I tried to get to sleep again.

But I kept hearing noises in the jungle. I knew the screams were monkeys and parrots. But in the dark they sounded like dangerous animals moving through the long grass. It was hours before at last I fell asleep.

The next morning, I did not feel quite so ill. I knew somebody would come for the boat in the end, but they might not come for a long time. Perhaps days, perhaps weeks, perhaps they might not come at all. It would be silly to wait for somebody to come. I must begin walking again.

I could not take the boat. I did not have the strength to use it. In any case I did not want to steal the boat. It did not belong to me. I was going to walk and swim on down the river, as I had done before.

I found a tube of cream in the hut. I rubbed it on my cuts. I hoped it might get rid of the maggots, but that did not work. So I broke off a piece of bark. I used that to dig the maggots out. I dug out twenty-five of them in this way. Then I picked out some more with my teeth. My right arm was getting worse. I began to worry again. My arm would have to be cut off if I did not get help soon.

And then I heard voices. They were coming from the jungle.

10

It was real people after all this time. I saw them coming out of the trees. There were three men. They wore shorts and had bare feet. They were speaking in Spanish. Then they saw me. One of them spoke. 'Hey there,' he said. 'Who is sitting there?'

I had been in the jungle for ten and a half days. This was the first human voice I had heard in all that time. Suddenly I was no longer alone!

I had been lucky. I had been very lucky indeed. If I had not stopped at that place in order to sleep, I would not have seen the boat. If I had been swimming I would have gone right past the hut. The men only spent one night in that hut every three weeks. If I had come to the hut one day later, they would have missed me. Then I would have died. They told me there were no people living along this river.

The men were all half white and half Indian. They said they were out hunting but had caught nothing. They were woodcutters. They floated logs down the river to villages in the jungle.

I told them what had happened to me. But one of the men did not believe me. He did not believe that a small girl could live after an air-crash for ten and a half days in the jungle.

'But can't you see,' I said, 'I am ALIVE.'

They laughed at this and I laughed with them. But I still felt very ill and weak.

Then the men put me in an old blanket. They took the can of petrol and poured some on my arms and legs. After that they dug thirty fat maggots out of my flesh. The pain was terrible. Then they washed the cuts with salt water, and put cream on my bleeding skin.

Next they covered me with a mosquito net, and gave me something to eat. I was given fruit and porridge. But I was not hungry. I don't know why, but I was just not hungry. All the same I ate a little. I did not want to upset the woodcutters.

Then we set off again, and I knew that at last I was nearly home.

11

It was three days by boat to my father's house. But the men knew I was too ill to last such a trip. So they said they would take me to a village called Vista. This village had an air-strip for small planes, and a radio. They could radio for a plane to come and fetch me.

We set off by boat down the river. After a time we came to a small group of huts. Here I was given some tea and bananas.

I looked a terrible sight. My skirt was so ragged a man gave me a shirt and a pair of trousers to wear. People came running from every hut to see me. They stood staring at me as if I had come straight out of hell. I was dizzy and tired. I could not understand what all the fuss was about.

After a short rest we set off for Vista again. The sun was very hot by now. The men put a sheet over me. I lay at the bottom of the boat. I was dripping with sweat.

We reached Vista in the afternoon. Again crowds of people came running to see us. They stared at me.

They could not believe their eyes. But only one man spoke to me. They were afraid of me.

They were afraid because I looked so awful. My eyes were red and blood-shot. They were also puffed up. My face was cut and covered with bumps. My arms were all puffed up as well. They were covered with insect bites and holes from the maggots. I must have looked like something out of a nightmare.

I was taken into a small hut. Suddenly I began to shake all over. A terrible cramp came over my body. I could not walk a single step. I found it difficult to breathe.

They washed me in the medical room. They put something on my cuts to kill the maggots. Then they tied me to the bed. They were worried I might get a fever and go mad. They thought I might start ripping up my own cuts.

The plane came soon. It was the first plane I had seen since the crash. But I was not afraid when I was lifted on board, because I was so glad to be going home. In fact the pilot was a famous woman. She was Jerry Cobb, who had flown jet planes and big airliners. As we took off, I began to think of my father who would be waiting to meet me.

12

So that's how I came to be lying here in a house near a lake. There are palm trees all round, and my father's house is near. The doctors are treating me well and my father is often by my side.

We listened to the news on the radio. That was how we were sure that my mother had been killed in the crash. For the first time since the crash I started to cry, when I thought of my wonderful mother.

I have now heard all sorts of stories about the crash. Some say that other people were left alive after the crash. Others say that the plane blew up in mid-air. If this were so, then there were not likely to be many others left alive. There was a search party after the crash. They said that most of the dead bodies had been eaten to the bone by vultures, insects and maggots.

Now I must get better. I must not get upset by the past. I must not get upset about my terrors in the jungle and the death of my mother. I am still young. My life is ahead of me. I want to look after animals. I want to do the same sort of work as my parents. I am not afraid of feeding the animals and cleaning out the stalls. I am not afraid of hard work.

If I had been a lazy person, I would not be alive today.

13

Juliane was the only person who lived to tell this story, but other people did survive for a few days after the crash. They had been saved by the strong up-currents of wind as they fell, and by the seats they were still tied into.

But the search party could not get to them in time, because of the storm. The winds were still too strong for the helicopters to land.

So when the search party did reach the crash, they found about twelve bodies which had only just begun to rot. This showed that some people had been dead for only two or three days.

They found one woman's body in a stream. She had taken off most of her clothes. She must have been trying to cool off in the water. Her body had not yet been touched by animals. This showed she had only been dead for two days.

Then the search party broke into a cabin and found sixteen rotting bodies. The smell almost made them faint. But one woman was lying there on the seat. Her body had not begun to rot. Her head was resting on her arms. She was another who had only been dead for one or two days. She must have been alive in the cabin for days while the others were dying around her. She had just missed the search party.

But all these people were too badly hurt to get to safety. They were also not as good at staying alive as Juliane, who was so brave that she survived ten days alone in the jungle.

The Spirals Series

Stories

Jim Alderson
Crash in the Jungle
The Witch Princess

Jan Carew
Death Comes to the Circus
Footprints in the Sand

Barbara Catchpole
Laura Called
Nick

Susan Duberley
The Ring

Keith Fletcher and Susan Duberley
Nightmare lake

John Goodwin
Dead-end Job
Ghost Train

Paul Groves
Not that I'm Work-shy
The Third Climber

Anita Jackson
The Actor
The Austin Seven
Bennet Manor
Dreams
The Ear
A Game of Life or Death
No Rent to Pay

Paul Jennings
Eye of Evil
Maggot

Margaret Loxton
The Dark Shadow

Patrick Nobes
Ghost Writer

David Orme
City of the Roborgs
The Haunted Asteroids

Kevin Philbin
Summer of the Werewolf

Julie Taylor
Spiders

John Townsend
Back on the Prowl
Beware the Morris Minor
Fame and Fortune
Night Beast
SOS
A Minute to Kill

David Walke
Dollars in the Dust

Plays

Jan Carew
Computer Killer
No Entry
Time Loop

Julia Donaldson
Books and Crooks

John Godfrey
When I Count to Three

Nigel Grey
An Earwig in the Ear

Paul Groves
Tell Me Where it Hurts

Barbara Mitchelhill
Punchlines
The Ramsbottoms at Home

Madeline Sotheby
Hard Time at Batwing Hall

John Townsend
A Bit of a Shambles
Breaking the Ice
Cheer and Groan
Clogging the Works
Cowboys, Jelly and Custard
The End of the Line
Hanging by a Fred
The Lighthouse Keeper's Secret
Making a Splash
Murder at Muckleby Manor
Over and Out
Rocking the Boat
Spilling the Beans
Taking the Plunge

David Walke
The Bungle Gang Strike Again
The Good, the Bad and the Bungle
Package Holiday